LENT and EASTER WISDOM
from
FULTON J. SHEEN

LENT and EASTER WISDOM

from

FULTON J. SHEEN

Daily Scripture and Prayers
Together With Sheen's Own Words

A Redemptorist Pastoral Publication

Liguori
LIGUORI, MISSOURI

Imprimi Potest:
Richard Thibodeau, C.Ss.R.
Provincial, Denver Province
The Redemptorists

Published by Liguori Publications
Liguori, Missouri
www.liguori.org

Library of Congress Cataloging-in-Publication Data

    Lent and Easter wisdom from Fulton J. Sheen : daily scripture and prayers together with Sheen's own words.—1st ed.
        p. cm. — (A Redemptorist pastoral publication)
    ISBN 0-7648-1111-8
    1. Lent—Prayer-books and devotions—English. 2. Holy week—Prayer-books and devotions—English. 3. Easter—Prayer-books and devotions—English 4. Catholic Church—Prayer-books and devotions—English. I. Sheen, Fulton J. (Fulton John), 1895–1979. II. Series.

BX2170.L4L45   2004
242'.34—dc22
2003065651

Liguori Publications, a nonprofit corporation, is an apostolate of the Redemptorists. To learn more about the Redemptorists, visit *Redemptorists.com.*

Printed in the United States of America
11 10 09 08 07   7 6 5 4 3

Contents

Epigraph

THERE HAS NEVER yet been a bomb invented that is half so powerful as one mortal sin—and yet there is no positive power in sin, only negation, only annihilation.

THOMAS MERTON
THE SEVEN STOREY MOUNTAIN

Introduction

MOST CATHOLICS seem to be aware of the forty-day period before the feast of Easter. Lent, which comes from the Anglo-Saxon word *lencten*, meaning "spring," is a time marked by particular rituals, such as the reception of ashes on Ash Wednesday or the decision to "give up French fries" as a Lenten practice. Is Lent broader than just these practices which seem to be left over from another era?

A BRIEF HISTORY OF LENT

In the first three centuries of the Christian experience, preparation for the Easter feast usually covered a period of one or two days, perhaps a week at the most. Saint Irenaeus of Lyons even speaks of a *forty-hour* preparation for Easter.

The first reference to Lent as a period of forty days' preparation occurs in the teachings of the First Council of Nicaea in A.D. 325 and, by the end of the fourth century, a Lenten period of forty days was established and accepted.

In its early development, Lent quickly became associated with the sacrament of baptism, since Easter was the great baptismal feast. Those who were preparing to be baptized participated in the season of Lent in preparation for the reception of the sacrament of baptism. Eventually, those who were already baptized considered it important to join those candidates preparing for baptism in their preparations for Easter. The customs and practices of Lent as we know them today soon took hold.

LENT AS A JOURNEY

Lent is often portrayed as a journey, from one point in time to another point in time. The concept of journey is obvious for those experiencing the Rite of Christian Initiation of Adults (RCIA), the program of baptismal preparation conducted in most parishes during the season of Lent.

But Lenten preparation is not limited to those who are preparing to be baptized and join the Church. For many Catholics, Lent is a journey that is measured from Ash Wednesday through Easter Sunday, but, more accurately, Lent is measured from Ash Wednesday to the beginning of the period of time known as the Triduum.

Triduum begins after the Mass on Holy Thursday, continues through Good Friday, and concludes with the Easter Vigil on Holy Saturday. Lent officially ends with the proclamation of the *Exscultet*, "Rejoice O Heavenly Powers," during the Mass of Holy Saturday.

By whatever yardstick the journey is measured, it is not only the period of time that is important but the essential experiences of the journey that are necessary for a full appreciation of what is being celebrated.

The Lenten journey is also a process of spiritual growth and, as such, presumes movement from one state of being to another state. For example, some people may find themselves troubled and anxious at the beginning of Lent as a result of a life choice or an unanswered question, and, at the end of Lent, they may fully expect a sense of conversion, a sense of peace, or perhaps simply understanding and acceptance. In this sense, Lent is a movement from one point of view to another or, perhaps, from one interpretation of life to a different interpretation.

Scripture, psalms, prayers, rituals, practices, and penance are the components of the Lenten journey. Each component, tried and tested by years of tradition, is one of the "engines" that drives the season and which brings the weary traveler to the joys of Easter.

PENITENTIAL NATURE OF LENT

A popular understanding of Lent is that it is a penitential period of time during which people attempt to become more sensitive to the role of sin in their lives. Lenten sermons will speak of personal sin, coming to an awareness of the sins of others and the effect such sin might have, and, finally, the sin that can be found within our larger society and culture. Awareness of sin, however, is balanced by an emphasis on the love and acceptance that God still has for humanity, despite the sinful condition in which we still find ourselves.

Awareness of sin and the need for penance is emphasized through the practice of meditation on the Passion of the Lord, his suffering, and his death. There is also a traditional concern for the reception of the sacrament of reconciliation during Lent. Originally, the sacrament of reconciliation was celebrated before Lent began, the penance imposed on Ash Wednesday, and the prescribed penance was performed during the entire forty-day period.

SUMMONS TO PENITENTIAL LIVING

"Jesus came to Galilee, proclaiming the good news of God, and saying, 'The time is fulfilled, and the kingdom of God has come near; repent, and believe in the good news'" (Mk 1:14–15). This call to conversion announces the solemn opening of Lent. Participants are marked with ashes, and the words, "Repent, and believe in the good news," are prayed. This blessing is understood as a personal acceptance of the desire to take on the life of penance for the sake of the Gospel.

✝ For forty days, the example of Jesus in the desert fasting and praying is imitated. It is time to center attention on conversion. During Lent, the expectation is to examine our lives and, through the practice of prayer, fasting, and works of charity, seek to conform our lives to Christ's. For some, this conversion will be a turning from sin to grace. For others, it will be a gracious turning toward the mystery of God in Christ. Whatever the pattern chosen by a particular pilgrim for an observance of Lent, it is hoped that this book will provide a useful support in the effort.

PART I

~~~~~~

READINGS *for* LENT

Ash Wednesday

A NEW START

God, in his great mercy, has instituted the sacrament by which the sins committed after baptism may be remitted. No human being would ever have thought of this sacrament [of reconciliation] for it is something like a resurrection; we rise after we are dead. It is a journey back again to God. It enables us to get rid of infections before they become chronic diseases and epidemics. The sacrament of reconciliation is the inflowing of God's mercy, an opportunity for the increase of the grace of Calvary. It is a medicine for the soul, the healing of our wounds, a homecoming, an undoing of the past; an opportunity to get a fresh start in life, another bath, a kind of secondary baptism.

FULTON J. SHEEN, AUDIO TAPE, "SIN"

CHANGE OF HEART

Yet even now, says the LORD,
    return to me with all your heart,
with fasting, with weeping, and with mourning;
    rend your hearts and not your clothing.
Return to the LORD, your God,
    for he is gracious and merciful,
slow to anger, and abounding in steadfast love,
    and relents from punishing....
Call a solemn assembly;
    gather the people.
Sanctify the congregation;
    assemble the aged;
gather the children,
    even infants at the breast....
Between the vestibule and the altar,
    let the priests, the ministers of the LORD, weep.
Let them say, "Spare your people, O LORD."

JOEL 2:12–17

PRAYER

Lord, encourage us in this season of Lent to arise from the sickness of sin. As the cross of ashes is traced on our foreheads on this day, may we be reminded that Christ's conquest of death is our entrance to a new life. We pray that our observance of this season will show us worthy of his sacrifice. Amen.

LENTEN ACTION

As Peter Chrysologus writes, "Fasting is the soul of prayer." Select a habit or attitude from which to "fast" as part of your spiritual program for Lent.

DAY 2

Thursday After Ash Wednesday

IT'S NOT MY FAULT!

$\mathcal{T}$he worse sinners are nice people who, by denying sin, make the cure of sin impossible. Sin is very serious, but it is more serious to deny sin. That is why those who very often deny sin become scandal mongers, tale bearers, and hypercritics, because they have to project their real guilt outside of themselves to others. And this gives them, also, a great illusion of goodness. It will be found generally true that the increase of fault finding is in direct proportion to the denial of sin.

FULTON J. SHEEN, AUDIO TAPE, "SIN"

FROM DEATH TO LIFE

You…must consider yourselves dead to sin and alive to God in Christ Jesus….[Do not let sin exercise dominion in your mortal bodies, to make you obey their passions.]No longer present your members to sin as instruments of wickedness, but present yourselves to God as those who have been brought from death to life.

ROMANS 6:11–13

PRAYER

Lord Creator, we take this first step of our Lenten journey by admitting our sinfulness. We work to remove the ashes of sin from our souls. Shine the light of your grace on us so that we may be wise people in your service. Amen.

LENTEN ACTION

Eat an apple today as a symbol of Adam and Eve's expulsion from the Garden of Eden.

DAY 3

Friday After Ash Wednesday

WHY SHOULD WE PRAY?

Well, why breathe? We have to take in fresh air and get rid of bad air; we have to take in new power and get rid of our old weaknesses....Just as a battery sometimes runs down and needs to be charged, so we have to be renewed in spiritual vigor. Our Blessed Lord said: "Without me you can do nothing." O yes, we can eat and drink, and we can sin, but we cannot do anything toward our supernatural merit and heaven without him.

FULTON J. SHEEN, AUDIO TAPE, "PRAYER IS A DIALOGUE"

Moving Mountains

Peter then said to him [Jesus], "Rabbi, look! The fig tree that you cursed has withered." Jesus answered, "Have faith in God. Truly, I tell you, if you say to this mountain, 'Be taken up and thrown into the sea,' and if you do not doubt in your heart, but believe that what you say will come to pass, it will be done for you. So I tell you, whatever you ask for in prayer, believe that you have received it, and it will be yours."

MARK 11:21–24

Prayer

God of Grace, inspire our prayer during this Lent and bless our intentions. Hear our prayer and do not avoid or forget us in our hour of need. Amen.

Lenten Action

Dedicate a particular time for prayer and decide on a specific prayer routine. Pray that prayer becomes a habit, a familiar path, not an occasional activity.

DAY 4

Saturday After Ash Wednesday

SELF-DISCIPLINE

*M*ortification is good, but only when it is done out of love of God, A "saint" who spends his [or her] life sizzling on hot coals or reclining on railroad spikes would never be canonized by the Church. Asceticism for asceticism's sake is actually a form of egotism, for self-discipline is only a *means*, the end of which is greater love of God. Any form of asceticism that disrupted charity would be wrong—this was the mistake of the monk who decided to live only on crusts and upset the whole monastery, turning it into one vast crust hunt to satisfy his idiosyncrasies.

FULTON J. SHEEN, *PEACE OF SOUL*

TASTE THE GOODNESS OF THE LORD

Rid yourselves, therefore, of all malice, and all guile, insincerity, envy, and all slander. Like newborn infants, long for the pure, spiritual milk, so that by it you may grow into salvation—if indeed you have tasted that the Lord is good.

1 PETER 2:1–3

PRAYER

Lord of Love, give us the self-discipline of the gardener who prunes the rose bush to make it bloom more beautifully. Let us likewise sacrifice our pleasures this Lent in order to groom our souls for eternal life. Amen.

LENTEN ACTION

What personal pleasure will I get along without for the betterment of my soul? Think of this denial as an exchange: self-discipline in exchange for our soul, in exchange for spiritual progress.

DAY 5

First Sunday of Lent

HEART MEETS HEART

*T*he nature of giving is best illustrated in the life of Our Blessed Lord, who one day was approached by a leper who asked for healing. The gospel tells us that Our Lord stretched forth his hand and touched the leper. Jesus could have healed without the touch, as he healed the servant of the centurion at a distance. Why, then, in the face of one of life's greatest miseries and a disease from which the healthy often recoil, did the Lord cure with a touch…?

The Son of God Made Man touched the leper in order to annihilate distance between the Giver and the receiver, between the Lover and the beloved, to prove sympathy by contact, to identify himself with the woes of others.

FULTON J. SHEEN, *FOOTPRINTS IN A DARKENED FOREST*

Healing Faith

As Jesus went on from there, two blind men followed him, crying loudly, "Have mercy on us, Son of David!" When he entered the house, the blind men came to him; and Jesus said to them, "Do you believe that I am able to do this?" They said to him, "Yes, Lord." Then he touched their eyes and said, "According to your faith let it be done to you." And their eyes were opened.

MATTHEW 9:27–30

Prayer

Christ Our Redeemer, in faith let us pray that we will be healed of our failings even though we can only touch you with our hearts and not with our hands. Do not let us doubt as did Thomas. Turn our weaknesses into strengths for your sake. Amen.

Lenten Action

The forty days of Lent commemorate the forty days that Jesus remained in the desert where the angels waited on him during his temptations by Satan. Let us begin our Lent by serving as "angels" to those around us who are tempted, since the devil, according to Saint Thomas Aquinas, is more disposed to attack those who are alone and have no support. Be a good companion if only for the day.

DAY 6

Monday of the First Week of Lent

THE FIRES OF ENTHUSIASM

Decisions and resolutions taken during an enthusiastic moment mean little unless tested by time and by waiting. At the beginning of the public life of Our Lord, when many disciples wished to follow him, he refused to accept them. The immediate request for places on the right and left side of the kingdom by James and John he ordered tested by the ability to bear sacrifice and to drink the cup of his Passion and Crucifixion. When, after multiplying the bread, the multitude wished to make him a bread king, Our Lord fled into the mountains alone. Economic kingships last only while the bread is plentiful. It is always a good policy never to choose the most enthusiastic person in a gathering as a leader. Wait to see how much wood there is for the flame.

FULTON J. SHEEN, *GUIDE TO CONTENTMENT*

12

"MY TIME HAS NOT YET COME"

Jesus went about in Galilee. He did not wish to go about in Judea because the Jews were looking for an opportunity to kill him. Now the Jewish festival of Booths was near. So his brothers said to him, "Leave here and go to Judea so that your disciples also may see the works you are doing; for no one who wants to be widely known acts in secret. If you do these things, show yourself to the world." (For not even his brothers believed in him.) Jesus said to them, "My time has not yet come, but your time is always here. The world cannot hate you, but it hates me because I testify against it that its works are evil."

JOHN 7:1–7

PRAYER

Lord of Spirit and Life, make us worthy of acceptance as your disciples, even though we are still sinners. Enrich us by our observance of this Lent and bring us back to your wisdom. Let us be as tested and true followers, not as mere dry wood rapidly consumed by the fire. Amen.

LENTEN ACTION

Today and for the rest of Lent, perform your good works in secret and without seeking congratulations or honor.

DAY 7

Tuesday of the First Week of Lent

RETALIATION

*W*hy should we turn the other cheek? Because hate multiplies like a seed. If one preaches hate and violence to ten men in a row, and tells the first to strike the second, and the second to strike the third, the hatred will envelop all ten. The only way to stop this hate is for one man to turn his other cheek. Then the hatred ends. It is never passed on. Absorb violence for the sake of the Savior, who will absorb sin and die for it. The Christian law is that the innocent shall suffer for the guilty. Thus Jesus would have us do away with adversaries, because when no resistance is offered, the adversary is conquered by a superior moral power.

FULTON J. SHEEN, *THE LIFE OF CHRIST*

GO THE SECOND MILE

Jesus taught them, saying, "You have heard that it was said, 'An eye for an eye and a tooth for a tooth.' But I say to you, Do not resist an evildoer. But if anyone strikes you on the right cheek, turn the other also; and if anyone wants to sue you and take your coat, give your cloak as well; and if anyone forces you to go one mile, go also the second mile."

MATTHEW 5:38–41

PRAYER

Dear Father, may we go the extra mile in your service during this Lent. Amen.

LENTEN ACTION

Be prepared for setbacks on this Lenten journey. Accept them in stride and find a practical way to overcome any obstacles. Retain spiritual wholeheartedness.

DAY 8

Wednesday of the First Week of Lent

LENIENCY OF GOD

When you fail to measure up to your Christian privilege, be not discouraged for discouragement is a form of pride. The reason you are sad is because you looked to yourself and not to God; to your failing, not to his love. You will shake off your faults more readily when you love God than when you criticize yourself....You have always the right to love him in your heart even though you do not love him in your acts....

Do not fear God for perfect love casts our fear. God is biased in your favor....God is more lenient than you because he is perfectly good and, therefore, loves you more. Be bold enough, then, to believe that God is on your side, even when you forget to be on his.

FULTON J. SHEEN, *PREFACE TO RELIGION*

LOVE OF GOD

God is love, and those who abide in love abide in God, and God abides in them. Love has been perfected among us in this: that we may have boldness on the day of judgment, because as he is, so are we in this world. There is no fear in love, but perfect love casts out fear; for fear has to do with punishment, and whoever fears has not reached perfection in love.

1 JOHN 4:16–18

PRAYER

O Lord, save us from ourselves as our own worst enemies. Help us to shake off our faults as your apostles shook the dust off their sandals. Give us the grace of perseverance so that we do not abandon our Lenten observance and settle for less than we can be. Amen.

LENTEN ACTION

As Blessed John of Vollombrosa declared, "I am resolved, with the help of Christ, to waste no more time." Plan your Lenten observances so as to make the best use of this time.

Thursday of the First Week of Lent

THE SWORD OF PRAYER

*G*od will not do what we can very well do for ourselves; he will not make a harvest grow without our planting the seed.…But there must be the preparation for God's help through the asking, the seeking, and the knocking.…Millions of favors are hanging from Heaven on silken cords—prayer is the sword that will cut them. "See where I stand at the door, knocking; if anyone listens to my voice and opens the door, I will come in to visit him, and take my supper with him" (Rev 3:20).

FULTON J. SHEEN, *LIFT UP YOUR HEART*

BREAD, NOT STONES

"Ask, and it will be given you; search, and you will find; knock, and the door will be opened for you. For everyone who asks receives, and everyone who searches, finds, and for everyone who knocks, the door will be opened. Is there anyone among you who, if your child asks for bread, will give a stone? Or if the child asks for a fish, will give a snake? If you then, who are evil, know how to give good gifts to your children, how much more will your Father in heaven give good things to those who ask him!

MATTHEW 7:7–11

PRAYER

God, who is both the door and the one who stands behind the door waiting for our knock, pour your blessings out on us. We acknowledge our dependence on you, we ask that you rid us of our selfishness and egoism. Let us know and understand the peace and joy that comes with surrender to your will. Amen.

LENTEN ACTION

Change the focus of your prayer of petition from "Dear God, give me your favors" to "Dear God, make me a more faithful and loving child of your creation."

DAY 10

Friday of the First Week of Lent

GOD LOVES YOU

*I*f you want to know about God, there is only one way to do it: get down on your knees. You can make his acquaintance by investigation, but you can win his love only by loving....

Most people who deny God do not do so because their reason tells them there is no God, for how could reason witness against Reason? Their denial is rather because of "wishful thinking." They feel they would be happier if there were no God, for then they could do as they pleased...

Think a little less about whether you deserve to be loved by him; he loves you even though you are not deserving. It is his love alone that will make you deserving. Most of us are unhappy because we never give God a chance to love us; we are in love only with ourselves.

FULTON J. SHEEN, *PREFACE TO RELIGION*

Evil Suppresses Truth

For the wrath of God is revealed from heaven against all ungodliness and wickedness of those who by their wickedness suppress the truth. For what can be known about God is plain to them, because God has shown it to them. Ever since the creation of the world his eternal power and divine nature, invisible though they are, have been understood and seen through the things he has made. So they are without excuse; for though they knew God, they did not honor him as God or give thanks to him, but they became futile in their thinking, and their senseless minds were darkened. Claiming to be wise, they became fools.

ROMANS 1:18–22

Prayer

Father, keep your children from foolish ways during this Lent and always. Purge us of our love of, and preoccupation with, ourselves and make sure that we give you a chance to love us fully. Amen.

Lenten Action

Honor God by making sure that you kneel in prayer today.

DAY 11

Saturday of the First Week of Lent

ROMANCE OF REPETITION

*T*here was a beautiful monotony in the story of Christ's life; thirty years obeying—not one year; three years teaching—not one year; three hours redeeming—not one hour. And as he lived he taught, and all his wisdom could be summed up in the words, "Do it again." There was the monotony of sacrifice—"Take up your cross daily, and follow me"; the monotony of kindness—"If one strike thee on thy right cheek, turn to him also the other"; the monotony of mercy—"How often should we forgive? Till seven times? Aye, till seventy times seven times";...the monotony of sacrificial thoughtfulness—"Do this in commemoration of me"; the monotony of prayer—"And he prayed for the third time."

FULTON J. SHEEN, *MANIFESTATIONS OF CHRIST*

The Goal of a Christian

Rejoice in the Lord always; again I will say, Rejoice. Let your gentleness be known to everyone. The Lord is near. Do not worry about anything, but in everything by prayer and supplication with thanksgiving let your requests be made known to God.

PHILIPPIANS 4:4–6

Prayer

God of Ever-Monotonous Creation, keep us focused on our goal of eternity. Bring us closer to union with our Lord and help us to repeat acts of faith, hope, charity, prudence, justice, fortitude, and love, making us continue week after week and year after year in order to find joyous monotony in your service. Amen.

Lenten Action

Find an opportunity for optimism today, even in the face of worldly pessimism.

﹏﹏ DAY 12 ﹏﹏

Second Sunday of Lent

THE VALUE OF DARKNESS

*D*arkness may be creative, for it is there that God plants his seeds to grow and his bulbs to flower. It is at night that the sheep that are scattered are gathered into the unity of the sheepfold, when the children come home to their mother and the soul back to God. Daylight deceives us, but as we awake at night, we get a new sense of values; darkness seems to tell the awful truth. As the psalmist puts it: "Day to day pours forth speech and night to night declares knowledge" (Ps 19:2). Night has its wonders, as well as day; darkness is not final, except to those who are without God.

FULTON J. SHEEN, *CROSS-WAYS*

GOD'S COVENANT WITH ABRAHAM

As the sun was going down, a deep sleep fell upon Abram, and a deep and terrifying darkness descended upon him. Then the LORD said to Abram, "Know this for certain, that your offspring shall be aliens in a land that is not theirs, and shall be slaves there, and they shall be oppressed for four hundred years; but I will bring judgment on the nation that they serve, and afterward they shall come out with great possessions.... When the sun had gone down and it was dark, a smoking fire pot and a flaming torch passed between these pieces [of animal sacrifice]. On that day the LORD made a covenant with Abram."

GENESIS 15:12–14, 17–18

PRAYER

Glorious Father, in the desert and darkness of this Lent, let us see the glory of the resurrected Christ. Let light shine out of the darkness of our sins. Amen.

LENTEN ACTION

Turn on a night light or light a votive candle to remind you of the illumination each Christian should provide in a darkened and sinful world.

⁂⁂⁂ DAY 13 ⁂⁂⁂⁂⁂⁂⁂⁂⁂⁂⁂⁂⁂⁂⁂⁂

Monday of the Second Week of Lent

JUDGING OTHERS

*J*udging our fellow human beings is as perplexing as the perceiving of colors on a spinning top. When a person is at rest, or in a fixed state,…we think we can very well judge his character. But when we see him in the whirl and motion of everyday life…all his goodness and badness blur into indistinctness. There is so much goodness at one moment, badness at another, sin in one instance, virtue in another, sobriety at one point, excess in another, that it is well to leave the judgment to God.…

The way we judge others is very often the judgment which we pronounce on ourselves.…Every dramatist, scriptwriter, novelist, and essayist who attacks the moral law has already lived against it in his own life. These men may not know it, but in their writings they are penning their own autobiography.…

FULTON J. SHEEN, *GUIDE TO CONTENTMENT*

MEASURE FOR MEASURE

Jesus said, "Do not judge, and you will not be judged; do not condemn, and you will not be condemned. Forgive, and you will be forgiven; give, and it will be given to you. A good measure, pressed down, shaken together, running over, will be put into your lap; for the measure you give will be the measure you get back."

LUKE 6:37–38

PRAYER

Merciful Lord, cleanse our hearts and souls from the fetters of resentment and the bitterness of brooding over wrongs, real or imagined. Keep us, if only for today, from the temptation to appoint ourselves judges of others. Let us recognize that condemnation of others is always sparked by selfishness, and let us remember that you are our only sure and final judge. Amen.

LENTEN ACTION

Joyfully abstain from all judgments of people, events, or things for at least one day. Contribute to your parish or local charity for each lapse.

DAY 14

Tuesday of the Second Week of Lent

HUMILITY ADDS CHARACTER

There are certain psychological and spiritual conditions which are essential for the discovery of truth, and the most important of these is the virtue of humility. Humility is not a want of moral force; rather humility is a recognition of the truth about ourselves. To explore the Truth in all its complexity there must come moments when we confess ignorance, when we frankly admit that we were mistaken or bigoted or prejudiced. These admissions are painful, but they actually enrich character just as much as all approximations to falsehood forfeit it. If we are proud, covetous, conceited, selfish, lustful, constantly wanting our own way, it is far better to come face to face with our own ugliness than live in a fool's paradise.

FULTON J. SHEEN, *WAY TO INNER PEACE*

Uprooting the Proud

Arrogance is hateful to the Lord
and to mortals,
and injustice is outrageous to both....
How can dust and ashes be proud?
Even in life the human body decays....
The beginning of human pride is to forsake the Lord;
the heart has withdrawn from its Maker....
The Lord overthrows the thrones of rulers,
and enthrones the lowly in their place.

SIRACH 10:7, 9, 12, 14

Prayer

God of Goodness, let our planting be in the good earth of humility and not in the arrogant heights of snobbishness and pride. Make us always mindful that we are but ashes easily blown away in the slightest breeze. Amen.

Lenten Action

Ashes are a symbol of penance and death. Originally, ashes were a sign of individual penance, but the ashes of the first day of Lent are a public sign and signify our solidarity in sin with our fellow Christians. Place a small dish of ashes on your nightstand, desk, or dinner table, reminding you to face up to one character flaw just for today.

DAY 15

Wednesday of the Second Week of Lent

REJECTION OF THE LIGHT

When the Light shines on the souls of humans and reveals their sins, they hate it just as the bank robber hates the searchlight the police have turned on him. The truth which Jesus brought, humans recognized as a claim on their allegiance, because they were made for it; but since they had perverted their natures by evil behavior, his truth stirred their consciences and they despised it. All their habits of life, their dishonesties, and baser passions roused them in violent opposition to that Light.

FULTON J. SHEEN, *THE LIFE OF CHRIST*

SALT AND LIGHT

Jesus taught them, saying, "You are the salt of the earth; but if salt has lost its taste, how can its saltiness be restored? It is no longer good for anything, but is thrown out and trampled under foot.

"You are the light of the world. A city built on a hill cannot be hid. No one after lighting a lamp, puts it under the bushel basket, but on the lampstand, and it gives light to all in the house. In the same way, let your light shine before others, so that they may see your good works and give glory to your Father in heaven."

MATTHEW 5:13–16

PRAYER

Lord of Light, keep our eyes and hearts adjusted so that we are not blinded to your word. Make us always welcome your light, even when it becomes a threat to the recognition of our sins. Purify us by the light of your grace and prevent us from shutting out your light and turning against your mercy. Amen.

LENTEN ACTION

Forego salt (or salty food) or butter at one meal or for the entire day. Let the absence of this seasoning remind you of just how significant God's grace is to all people.

DAY 16

Thursday of the Second Week of Lent

YAKKETY, YAK

This is probably the most talkative age in the history of the world—not only because we have more mechanical devices to diffuse our talking but also because we have little inside our minds that did not come from the world outside our minds. …There are few listeners, although Saint Paul tells us that "faith comes from hearing." If the bodies of most of us were fed as little as the mind, they would soon starve to death. Hyperactivity and love of noise and chatter characterize our age, as a compensation for the profound distrust human beings have of themselves.

FULTON J. SHEEN, *LIFT UP YOUR HEART*

ATTENTION, PLEASE

Jesus took with him Peter and James and his brother John and led them up a high mountain, by themselves. And he was transfigured before them, and his face shone like the sun, and his clothes became dazzling white. Suddenly there appeared to them Moses and Elijah, talking with [Jesus]. Then Peter said to Jesus, "Lord, it is good for us to be here; if you wish, I will make three dwellings here, one for you, one for Moses, and one for Elijah." While he was still speaking, suddenly a bright cloud overshadowed them, and from the cloud a voice said, "This is my Son, the Beloved; with him I am well pleased; listen to him!"

MATTHEW 17:1–5

PRAYER

O God, who has created our free will, help us hear and heed your voice that is within us. Help us to recognize and accept your truth in spite of the many reasons we put forth to deny your healing power and your message of salvation. Amen.

LENTEN ACTION

On this day, practice true listening, receiving the words of others and processing before even thinking of how to phrase an answer.

DAY 17

Friday of the Second Week of Lent

THE VINEYARD OF SOULS

*L*ove has three and only three intimacies: speech, vision, and touch. These three intimacies God has chosen to make his love intelligible to our poor hearts. God has spoken: He told us that he loves us: That is Revelation. God has been seen: That is the Incarnation. God has touched us by his grace: That is Redemption. Well indeed, therefore, may he say: "What more could I do for my vineyard than I have done? What other proof could I give of my love than to exhaust myself in the intimacies of love? What else could I do to show that my own Sacred Heart is not less generous than your own?"

If we answer these questions aright, then we will begin to repay love with love....Then we will return speech with speech which will be our prayer; vision with vision which will be our faith; touch with touch which will be our communion.

FULTON J. SHEEN, *THE ETERNAL GALILEAN*

The True Vine

Jesus answered, "I am the true vine, and my Father is the vinegrower. He removes every branch in me that bears no fruit. Every branch that bears fruit he prunes to make it bear more fruit. You have already been cleansed by the word that I have spoken to you. Abide in me as I abide in you. Just as the branch cannot bear fruit by itself unless it abides in the vine, neither can you unless you abide in me."

JOHN 15:1–4

Prayer

Keeper of the Vineyard, the vine which grows to life through death on the cross, watch over us, and protect us. Make us ever aware of the needs of those who live around us. Let us help them to grow vigorously by the light of your Resurrection. Amen.

Lenten Action

Use one of the three intimacies of love (speech, vision, or touch) to demonstrate charity and community to another. Say the short prayer "O Sacred Heart of Jesus, be my salvation" at points throughout the day.

☩☩☩ DAY 18

Saturday of the Second Week of Lent

NATURAL KINDNESS

*B*ecause kindness is related to love, it follows that the kind person loves another not for the pleasure the other person gives, not because the other person can do us a kindness in return, but because the other person is lovable in himself. The basic reason why everyone is lovable is because God made him. If we were evolved from the beast, none of us would be deserving of any love....

To a great extent the world is what we make it. We get back what we give. If we sow hate, we reap hate; if we scatter love and gentleness we harvest love and happiness. Other people are like a mirror which reflects back on us the kind of image we cast. The kind person bears with the infirmities of others, never magnifies trifles, and avoids a spirit of fault finding.

FULTON J. SHEEN, *WAY TO HAPPINESS*

KINDNESS TO ALL

Remind them of this, and warn them before God that they are to avoid wrangling over words, which does no good but only ruins those who are listening. Do your best to present yourself to God as one approved by him, a worker who has no need to be ashamed, rightly explaining the word of truth....

Shun youthful passions and pursue righteousness, faith, love, and peace, along with those who call on the Lord from a pure heart.

2 TIMOTHY 2:14–15, 22

PRAYER

Father of Light and Ever-Changeless God, open our hearts to your unlimited truth and let us show by our deeds, and not just by our words, that we are workers in the service of your Truth. Amen.

LENTEN ACTION

Bear with those who irritate you if only for today. Make every effort not to magnify the importance of the "small stuff."

DAY 19

Sunday of the Third Week of Lent

TRUE PROGRESS

The Church believes that a holy hour spent before the Blessed Sacrament does more good for the well-being of the world than whole days spent in talking about progress to the utter oblivion of the fact that the only true progress consists in the diminution of the traces of original sin; she believes that a penitent returning to God is of far more consequence than the cancellation of war debts; that an increase of sanctifying grace in a soul is of far more value than the increase of international credit; that a group of cloistered nuns in prayer are more effective in preserving world peace than a group of world politicians discussing peace to the forgetfulness of the Prince of Peace.

FULTON J. SHEEN, *MANIFESTATIONS OF CHRIST*

FOOLISH PROFIT

Jesus called the crowd with his disciples, and said to them, "If any want to become my followers, let them deny themselves and take up their cross and follow me. For those who want to save their life will lose it, and those who lose their life for my sake, and for the sake of the gospel, will save it. For what will it profit them to gain the whole world and forfeit their life?"

MARK 8:34–36

PRAYER

Lord Our God, speak to our hearts this Lent so that we may heed your voice and follow your commandments. Help us to turn away from useless things, no matter how attractive, and help us to serve you according to your plan. Amen.

LENTEN ACTION

Find time over the next days of Lent to spend a total of one hour in prayer in front of the Blessed Sacrament.

DAY 20

Monday of the Third Week of Lent

DIVINE CHEERFULNESS

Cheer may be natural, in which case it springs from an inborn vitality and zest for living. Even those who lack it can cultivate it to some extent, as marching music lessens fatigue.

But there is another kind of cheerfulness which is Divine in origin. Saint Paul bade others to have it as believing in God. This counsel he spoke to others in the midst of a storm at sea, promising them relief and rescue without loss of life. This kind of cheerfulness is found in Francis of Assisi, who expressed the joy of grace to his soul by song. Teresa of Ávila, who lived a life of great penance, was wont to pour out her joy in that inner world of spirituality by clapping her hands and dancing in the Spanish style. In the history of the world there never has been a sad saint, because sanctity and sadness are opposites.

FULTON J. SHEEN, *SIMPLE TRUTHS*

A Glad Heart

> *The heart changes the countenance,*
> *either for good or for evil.*
> *The sign of a happy heart is a cheerful face.*

SIRACH 13:25–26

Prayer

Saving God, we meditate on your wisdom and knowledge. Help us to find gladness and save us from the foolishness of sin. Amen.

Lenten Action

Smile sincerely at everyone you meet today.

DAY 21

Tuesday of the Third Week of Lent

THE STRONG AND THE WEAK

*T*here is a law that is not in nature, at least not in raw nature, namely, "We who are strong should bear the infirmities of the weak and not please ourselves." It is here that Christianity makes it most unique and distinctive pronouncement, and gives the supreme example of Divinity dying for the weakness and sinfulness of humanity. The Christian law is not "the survival of the fittest" but "the survival of the unfit."

FULTON J. SHEEN, *GUIDE TO CONTENTMENT*

GIVE TO THE WEAK

> *Give justice to the weak and the orphan;*
> *maintain the right of the lowly and the destitute.*
> *Rescue the weak and the needy;*
> *deliver them from the hand of the wicked.*

PSALM 82:3–4

PRAYER

Lord, grant us the grace to help the poor and the weak. Let us use our own strength to help those who suffer. Let not our own health blind us to those in pain. Amen.

LENTEN ACTION

Anonymously, give a helping hand to a person in your neighborhood, town, or city who needs immediate assistance.

DAY 22

Wednesday of the Third Week of Lent

THE DUTY OF WORK

*M*essages came to many in the Old Testament who were Shepherds. Moses received his credentials as the ambassador of the Most High…while feeding the flocks of Jethro. Abraham was a shepherd; so was David. Ezekiel, a prophet centuries before, had foretold, "Behold I will raise you a shepherd."

What interests us is that God called the shepherds while they were still at work doing their duty.…The best place in all the world to be for a higher summons is at a post of duty. Nowhere else are great temporal and spiritual blessings to be sought. When the Lord has a great gift or message to give to one of his children, he sends it to the place where that person ought to be found. It matters very little what we are doing; what does matter is that we are doing our duty. Sometimes the most humble occupations prepare for the greatest vocations.

FULTON J. SHEEN, *REJOICE*

LET EVERYONE WORK

Even when we [Paul, Sylvanus, and Timothy] were with you, we gave you this command: Anyone unwilling to work should not eat. For we hear that some of you are living in idleness, mere busybodies, not doing any work. Now such persons we command and exhort in the Lord Christ Jesus to do we their work quietly and to earn their own living.

2 THESSALONIANS 3:10–12

PRAYER

Faithful and Loving Father, let us find good in remembering you, even as we work and serve at our appointed posts. Let us draw energy from you for the sound fulfillment of our duties. Amen.

LENTEN ACTION

Like a faithful servant of the Lord, dedicate this day's work to the glory of God. Adopt some sign or symbol of this dedication.

Thursday of the Third Week of Lent

SILENCE

*T*he executioners expected Jesus to cry, for everyone pinned to the gibbet of the Cross had done it before him. Seneca wrote that those who were crucified cursed the day of their birth, the executioners, their mothers, and even spat on those who looked upon them. Cicero recorded that at times it was necessary to cut out the tongues of those who were crucified to stop their terrible blasphemies. Hence the executioners expected a word, but not the kind of word that they heard....Like some fragrant trees which bathe in perfume the very axe which gashes them, the great Heart on the Tree of Love poured out from its depths something less a cry than a prayer—the soft, sweet, low prayer of pardon and forgiveness.

FULTON J. SHEEN, *LIFE OF CHRIST*

CRUCIFIXION OF JESUS

Two others also, who were criminals, were led away to be put to death with him. When they came to the place that is called The Skull, they crucified Jesus there with the criminals, one on his right and one on his left. Then Jesus said, "Father, forgive them; for they do not know what they are doing."

LUKE 23:32–34

PRAYER

God of Justice, let us merit forgiveness for all our sins which just as surely fastened you to the cross as did the nails of the executioners. Amen.

LENTEN ACTION

Keep strict silence for fifteen minutes today.

Friday of the Third Week of Lent

THE FEAR OF SINNERS

*M*oses and Cain each hid his face from God. Moses hid his face because he could not bear to look upon such goodness; Cain hid his face because he could not bear to have Divine Goodness look at him. The sinner cannot bear to have the eyes of God upon him, for he does not want to know how wicked he is. But God cannot change his nature to make up for our perversity; it is the ego that must change its ways.

If an egotist really understood the psychology of the human mind, he would never be heard to say that God is wrathful—for such a statement publishes his sinfulness. As a brown-colored glass can make the water in it seem brown, although it is not, so the Love that waits for us, passing through our sinful lives, may seem like wrath and anger. A change in our behavior removes all the unhealthy fear of God.

FULTON J. SHEEN, *LIFT UP YOUR HEART*

EYES OF THE LORD

> *Come, O children, listen to me;*
> *I will teach you the fear the LORD.*
> *Which of you desires life,*
> *and covets many days to enjoy good?*
> *Keep your tongue from evil,*
> *and your lips from speaking deceit;*
> *Depart from evil and do good;*
> *seek peace and pursue it.*
> *The eyes of the LORD are on the righteous;*
> *and his ears are open to their cry.*
> *The face of the LORD is against evildoers,*
> *to cut off the remembrance of them from the earth.*
> *When the righteous cry for help the LORD hears,*
> *and rescues them from all their troubles.*

PSALM 34:11–17

PRAYER

God Our Father, look down from heaven and ransom us from our sins. We are confident that you will grant us what we ask according to your will. We trust in you for our daily bread and honor your name as we anticipate our home in heaven. Amen.

LENTEN ACTION

Put on an honest and peaceful face for the day. Do not dissemble and do not set your face in stone.

DAY 25

Saturday of the Third Week of Lent

DEATH OF LIGHT

*F*rom twelve o'clock until three o'clock there was an unearthly darkness that fell over the land, for nature, in sympathy with its Creator, refused to shed its light upon the crime of deicide. Humankind, having condemned the Light of the World, now lost the cosmic symbol of that Light, the sun. At Bethlehem, where he was born at midnight, the heavens were suddenly filled with light; at Calvary, when he entered into the ignominy of his crucifixion at midday, the heavens were bereaved of light.

FULTON J. SHEEN, *LIFE OF CHRIST*

DEATH OF JESUS

From noon on, darkness came over the whole land until three in the afternoon. And about three o'clock Jesus cried with a loud voice, "Eli, Eli, lema sabachthani?" that is, "My God, my God, why have you forsaken me?"

MATTHEW 27:45–46

PRAYER

Father of All Mercies, allow us to rejoice in our status as temples of God through baptism. We thank you for this gift of the water of life and salvation. Amen.

LENTEN ACTION

Find one instance among the pedestrian events of the day to affirm that God is ever among us, even in unseen ways.

DAY 26

Sunday of the Fourth Week of Lent

SEEING OURSELVES AS WE TRULY ARE

*A*long with silence, there must go a sense of the Presence of God. This means begging the Divine Light to illumine our hearts to see them not as we think we are, or as others think we are, but as we really are in the sight of God.

FULTON J. SHEEN, *SIMPLE TRUTHS*

THE LORD SEES OUR HEARTS

The LORD said to Samuel, "Fill your horn with oil and set out; I will send you to Jesse the Bethlehemite, for I have provided for myself a king among his sons."

When [Jesse and his sons] came, Samuel looked on Eliab and thought, "Surely the LORD's anointed is now before the LORD." But the LORD said to Samuel, "Do not look on his appearance or on the height of his stature, because I have rejected him; for the LORD does not see as mortals see; they look on the outward appearance, but the LORD looks on the heart."

1 SAMUEL 16:1, 6–7

PRAYER

God Our Father, cleanse our eyes of the dazzle brought on by the attraction of false appearances. Instead, this Lent, give us the vision to see people and things as they truly are. May our sacrifices contribute to our clarity of purpose and vision. Amen.

LENTEN ACTION

Set aside fifteen minutes this day for a meditative examination of conscience so that you may see yourself as God sees you.

DAY 27

Monday of the Fourth Week of Lent

ZEBRAS WITHOUT STRIPES?

Our Blessed Lord said that the Truth would make us free. By this he meant that only by obedience to the highest law and authority do we become free. Take an example from the realm of arts. If an artist in a fever of broad-mindedness and a desire to be free, chooses to paint a giraffe with a short neck, he will soon discover that he will not be free to paint a giraffe at all. If in a feverish love for the art of self-expression which obeys no law, he decides to paint a zebra without stripes, and a leopard without spots, and a triangle with four sides, he will soon discover that he is not free at all to paint even zebras, leopards, or triangles. It is only in obedience to law and authority and the inherent nature of things that we ever become free.

FULTON J. SHEEN, *MANIFESTATIONS OF CHRIST*

THE SON WHO MAKES US FREE

Jesus said to the Jews who had believed in him, "If you continue in my word, you are truly my disciples; and you will know the truth, and the truth will make you free."

JOHN 8:31–32

PRAYER

Lord God, grant us confidence in your fatherly love, ease our fears, and let us find the courage and conversion of true obedience. Amen.

LENTEN ACTION

Lent is customarily a time for making pilgrimages. Make a brief pilgrimage to a local shrine or church this day.

DAY 28

Tuesday of the Fourth Week of Lent

COME AND GO

Almost the first word of Our Lord's public life was "come" (Jn 1:39, Mk 1:17, Mt 4:18). The final word of his public life was "go" into the world (Jn 20:21, Mt 28:19, Acts 1:18). First one must come to him to learn, to be inspired, to find the ultimate goal of life, to discover meaning, purposes, the significance of justice and liberty. Then go among the nations, go to accomplish, go to serve, to wash feet, to feed the hungry, to establish equality, to pick up the wounded like good Samaritans.

FULTON J. SHEEN, *FOOTPRINTS IN A DARKENED FOREST*

Do Also to Others

During supper Jesus…got up from the table, took off his outer robe, and tied a towel around himself. Then he poured water into a basin and began to wash the disciples' feet and to wipe them with the towel that was tied around him.

After he had washed their feet, had put on his robe, and had returned to the table, he said to them, "Do you know what I have done to you? You call me Teacher and Lord—and you are right, for that is what I am. So if I, your Lord and Teacher, have washed your feet, you ought to wash one another's feet. For I have set you an example, that you also should do as I have done to you."

JOHN 13:3–5, 12–15

Prayer

Lord of Love and Sacrifice, whose washing of the feet of your disciples symbolizes our servant role as Christians, remind us also of the cleansing power of our baptism. By this sacrament we are washed clean of sin and admitted into salvation through Jesus' death. We accept this lot with humility. Amen.

Lenten Action

According to tradition, Pope Saint Gregory the Great washed the feet of thirteen people in memory of Christ's action on the night before he died and served them at table with bread and wine. Of the thirteen, twelve represent the apostles, and the other, who is always a young man, represents the angel who is said to have come to the table when Pope Gregory was serving it. In many Catholic countries, gifts were also given to the poor after the washing of the feet ceremony. Find some way to commemorate either of these two customs by giving gifts or by serving others at table.

DAY 29

Wednesday of the Fourth Week of Lent

HEROISM

*L*ove and sacrifice go together as with Elizabeth Pilenkoa, a young Russian who escaped Communism by fleeing to France. During the persecution of the Jews in World War II, she founded a convent as a haven for the Jews. When the Gestapo found her, she was led to the concentration camp at Ravensbruck. During two and a half years she saw a block of buildings erected which were actually gas chambers, though the prisoners were told they were to be hot baths for prisoners.

One day a number of women prisoners were lined up before the buildings. One girl became hysterical. Mother Maria, for that was her name as a nun, was not among those selected. To the girl who became hysterical she said, "Don't be frightened. I shall take your turn," knowing very well she was going to her death. It was Good Friday when she died.

FULTON J. SHEEN, *FOOTPRINTS IN A DARKENED FOREST*

Do Unto Others

Jesus said, "When the Son of Man comes in his glory, and all the angels with him, then he will sit on the throne of his glory....The king will say to those at his right hand, 'Come, you that are blessed by my Father, inherit the kingdom prepared for you from the foundation of the world; for I was hungry and you gave me food, I was thirsty and you gave me something to drink.'...Then the righteous will answer him, 'Lord, when was it that we saw you hungry and gave you food, or thirsty and gave you something to drink?...And the king will answer them, 'Truly I tell you, just as you did it to one of the least of these who are members of my family, you did it to me.'"

MATTHEW 25:31–40

Prayer

O God of the Entire Human Family, let us be worthy of the grace to stand at your right hand. When the hour comes, let us hear the voice of the Son of God and the Son of Man, who comes to exercise judgment. Prompt us always to do good deeds which ensure our passage from the slavery of sin to the resurrection of eternal life. Amen.

Lenten Action

Offer to pinch-hit for someone else who needs time to pray or to meditate. Alternately, pray on their behalf.

Thursday of the Fourth Week of Lent

DIVINE POWERLESSNESS

*W*e have this queer combination of Divine powerlessness in two verses of the Creed: "I believe in God, the Father Almighty" and then "in Jesus Christ who suffered under Pontius Pilate and was crucified." In the first instance, we have power; in the second instance, we have apparent powerlessness. The powerlessness of the Cross is no bogus promise to historical success. Therefore, on the Cross, Jesus' enemies sneered, "Come down, and we will believe." The test of power was the overcoming of the enemy who had nailed him. If he came down, he never would have saved us.

FULTON J. SHEEN, AUDIO TAPE, "CHRIST IN THE CREED"

SHEATHE THE SWORD

Judas, one of the twelve, arrived; with him was a large crowd with swords and clubs, from the chief priests and the elders of the people. Now the betrayer had given them a sign, saying, "The one I will kiss is the man; arrest him." At once he come up to Jesus and said, "Greetings, Rabbi!" and kissed him. Jesus said to him, "Friend, do what you are here to do." Then they came and laid hands on Jesus and arrested him. Suddenly one of those with Jesus put his hand on his sword, drew it, and struck the slave of the high priest, cutting off his ear. Then Jesus said to him, "Put your sword back into its place; for all who take the sword will perish by the sword."

MATTHEW 26:47–52

PRAYER

Blessed and gentle Lord, let us answer any violence, physical or emotional, that comes our way with the same humility that you demonstrated on the cross. May our daily actions diminish the power of evil in this world. Amen.

LENTEN ACTION

Take one peaceful action today, even if it is only symbolically turning off a violent television program or "tuning out" aggressive or hostile conversation.

DAY 31

Friday of the Fourth Week of Lent

RUBBISH PILES

*S*orrow [for sins] is an intention to abandon the ego. It is hard. Sometimes it is like being skinned alive, peeling away sins and getting rid of some of them, taking on a firm purpose of amendment....I believe that most people are sorry for their sins not just because they dread the loss of heaven and fear hell, it is because they have hurt our Lord. After all, it is the Cross that reveals the dimension of sin. No one ever thoroughly sees sin in its utter nakedness until he understands redemption. Take the errors and the stupidity and the crimes of every day. People summarize them by saying, "Oh, what a fool I made of myself!" There is a world of difference between that and, "Oh, what a sinner I am!"

FULTON J. SHEEN, AUDIO TAPE, "PENANCE"

REPENTANCE

If we say that we have fellowship with [God] while we are walking in darkness, we lie and do not do what is true; but if we walk in the light as he himself is in the light, we have fellowship with one another, and the blood of Jesus his Son cleanses us from all sin....If we confess our sins, he who is faithful and just will forgive us our sins and cleanse us from all unrighteousness.

1 JOHN 1:6–9

PRAYER

With Saint John Chrysostom, let us contemplate the "many wrongs that the cross has set right," and pray: Dear Lord, even by prayer and penance we cannot fathom the inscrutable way of the cross, but we seek faith that you will deliver us from our sins and rescue us from our wrongheadedness. Amen.

LENTEN ACTION

Say a fervent act of contrition today, perhaps one you create in your own words.

DAY 32

Saturday of the Fourth Week of Lent

DYING TO LIVE

*I*f a man is ever to enjoy communion with Christ, so as to have the blood of God running in his veins and the spirit of God throbbing in his soul, he must die to the lower life of the flesh. He must be born again….And hence the law of Calvary is the law of every Christian: unless there is the Cross there will never be the resurrection, unless there is the defeat of Calvary there will never be the victory of Easter, unless there are the nails there will never be the glorious wounds, unless there is the garment of scorn, there will never be the robes blazing like the sun, unless there is the crown of thorns there will never be the halo of light…for the law laid down at the beginning of time which shall be effective until time shall be no more, is that no one shall be crowned unless he has struggled and overcome.

FULTON J. SHEEN, *THE MORAL UNIVERSE*

CONQUERING THE WORLD

Everyone who believes that Jesus is the Christ has been born of God, and everyone who loves the parent loves the child. By this we know that we love the children of God, when we love God and obey his commandments. For the love of God is this, that we obey his commandments. And his commandments are not burdensome, for whatever is born of God conquers the world.

1 JOHN 5:1–4

PRAYER

O Great God, imprint the wounds of the cross on our hearts, so that we may use them effectively to overcome the destructive temptations of this world. Amen.

LENTEN ACTION

Take time to bind up the wounds of anger wherever you discover them today.

Sunday of the Fifth Week of Lent

WHERE WERE THE MEN ON CALVARY?

*B*ut though men failed in this crisis [of Calvary] there is no instance of a single woman failing. In the four trials the voice heard in [Christ's] defense was that of a woman, Claudia Procul, the wife of Pontius Pilate....

On Calvary it is woman who is fearless, for there are several of them at the foot of the Cross. Magdalene, among them as usual, is prostrate. But there is one whose courage and devotion was so remarkable that the Evangelist who was there indicated the detail that she was "standing." That woman was the mother of the man on the central cross.

Our Blessed Lord willed her presence there. Since he was the second Adam undoing the sin of the first, Mary would be the new Eve proclaiming the new race of the redeemed.

FULTON J. SHEEN, *THE NEW VIRTUES*

WOMEN OF JERUSALEM

A great number of people followed [Jesus on the way to Golgotha], and among them were women who were beating their breasts and wailing for him. But Jesus turned to them and said, "Daughters of Jerusalem, do not weep for me, but weep for yourselves and for your children. For the days are surely coming when they will say, 'Blessed are the barren, and the wombs that never bore, and the breasts that never nursed.'"

LUKE 23:27–29

PRAYER

Jesus, son of Mary, give us the grace to hold your Blessed Mother close to us, for what we love we become. Let her be our inspiration to prudence, faithfulness, and devotion. Let her always be Our Lady of Good Counsel. Amen.

LENTEN ACTION

Say the rosary today so that the Mother of our Lord will draw us closer to her son's Passion and death.

DAY 34

Monday of the Fifth Week of Lent

RIDDLE OF DEATH

*T*he only answer to the mystery of death would be for some-one to break the death barrier....Someone must pierce the mystery from within....And when that Death was preceded by poverty, hunger, thirst, hatred, miscarriage of justice, intellectual barbarisms, and scourgings, and the seeming abandonment of heaven, then I know that nothing that happens to me or anyone else can be worse and that it is eventually to be swallowed up in joy and peace....

Christ answers, "Can you not see that everything that touched you first touched me....I am in the midst of your sorrows; your tears run down my cheeks; your thirst is but an echo of my parched cry of the Cross. I died the very death that I conquered."

FULTON J. SHEEN, *FOOTPRINTS IN A DARKENED FOREST*

SCRIPTURE

Jesus said, "If I tell the truth, why do you not believe me? Whoever is from God hears the words of God. The reason you do not hear them is that you are not from God."

The Jews answered him, "Are we not right in saying that you are a Samaritan and have a demon?" Jesus answered, "I do not have a demon; but I honor my Father, and you dishonor me. Yet I do not seek my own glory; there is one who seeks it and he is the judge. Very truly, I tell you, whoever keeps my word will never see death."

JOHN 8:45–51

PRAYER

God of Life, remind us to face our own mortality daily by dying with you on the Cross. Help us prepare for the anguish and terror of our own death. Amen.

LENTEN ACTION

Actively try to love you neighbor just as Christ loved the Good Thief who was crucified with him.

DAY 35

Tuesday of the Fifth Week of Lent

REDEMPTION

*I*n the beautiful Divine economy of Redemption, the same three things which cooperated in the Fall shared in Redemption. For the disobedient man Adam, there was the obedient new Adam, Christ; for the proud woman Eve, there was the humble new Eve, the Virgin Mary; for the tree of the Garden, there was the tree of the Cross....Our Divine Lord in the state of his greatest humiliation, seeing all prophecies fulfilled, all foreshadowings realized, and all things done which were needful for the Redemption, uttered a cry of joy: "It is achieved."

FULTON J. SHEEN, *LIFE OF CHRIST*

DEATH OF JESUS

After this, when Jesus knew that all was now finished, he said (in order to fulfill the scripture), "I am thirsty." A jar full of sour wine was standing there. So they put a sponge full of the wine on a branch of hyssop and held it to his mouth. When Jesus had received the wine, he said, "It is finished." Then he bowed his head and gave up his spirit.

JOHN 19:28–30

PRAYER

Jesus Our Lord and Master, reach out your hand to greet us as we walk in your ways during this Lent. Let our works, however slender, let us reach the heavenly country. Amen.

LENTEN ACTION

Write the word *Maranatha* on a card to carry with you for the day. The word means "Lord, come," and signifies the belief that the Lord will return and, in a very real sense, comes into our life today.

DAY 36

Wednesday of the Fifth Week of Lent

THIRST

The God-Man, who threw the stars in their orbits and spheres into space, who "swung the earth as a trinket at his wrist," from whose fingertips tumbled planets and worlds, who might have said, "The sea is mine and with it the streams in a thousand valleys and the cataracts in a thousand hills," now asks man— man, a piece of his own handiwork—to help him. He asks man for a drink! Not a drink of earthly water, that is not what he meant, but a drink of love. "I thirst"—for love!

FULTON J. SHEEN, *THE ELECTRONIC CHRISTIAN*

SERMON ON THE MOUNT

When Jesus saw the crowds, he went up the mountain; and after he sat down, his disciples came to him. Then he began to speak, and taught them, saying, ... "Blessed are those who hunger and thirst for righteousness, for they will be filled."

MATTHEW 5:1, 6

PRAYER

Ever-living God, you have given us the water of life to drink through our risen Savior, who is Vine, Rock, Shepherd, Word. Make us thirst for him so we will turn aside from all lesser thirst. Amen.

LENTEN ACTION

Sacrifice your time today to spend it with others who need your company.

DAY 37

Thursday of the Fifth Week of Lent

BECOMING RICH IN HOLINESS

*S*anctity is not a question of relinquishing or giving up something for Christ: It is a question of exchange. In the spiritual world, I learn that there are many things that I can get along without, and as I grow in acquaintance with Christ, I find that I can get along without sin, but I cannot get along without his peace of conscience, and so I exchange one for the other. I find by a still deeper acquaintance that I can get along without the world's goods, but not without the wealth of Christ's grace, and so I exchange one for the other....Thus, the saint goes on exchanging one thing for another. And thus it is that in making himself poor, he becomes rich, and in making himself a slave, he becomes free.

FULTON J. SHEEN, *MANIFESTATIONS OF CHRIST*

WHAT WILL THEY GIVE?

Then Jesus told his disciples, ("*If any want to become my* ⊢ *followers, let them deny themselves and take up their cross and follow me.*) *For those who want to save their life will lose it, and those who lose their life for my sake will find it.* (*For what will it profit them if they gain the whole world but forfeit their life? Or what will they give in return for their life?*

MATTHEW 16:24–26

PRAYER

Father, help us to recognize all the benefits and blessings, temporal and spiritual, which you have given us. Let us consider how paltry our efforts at virtue are in the light of these gifts. Amen.

LENTEN ACTION

Follow the Stations of the Cross at home.

DAY 38

Friday of the Fifth Week of Lent

A PERSONAL INVITATION

✝ God solicits each of us by a dialogue no other soul can hear. His action on the soul is always for us alone. He sends no circular letters, uses no party lines. God never deals with crowds as crowds—they could give him only earthly glory—but what he wants is each soul's singular and secret fealty. He calls his sheep by name; he leaves the ninety-nine that are safe to find the one that is lost....Once the soul becomes conscious of the Divine Presence, it...whispers to itself: "This is a message sent to me and to no one else."

FULTON J. SHEEN, *LIFT UP YOUR HEART*

A Welcome for One Sinner

So Jesus told them this parable: "Which of you, having a hundred sheep and losing one of them, does not leave the ninety-nine in the wilderness and go after the one that is lost until he finds it? When he has found it, he lays it on his shoulders and rejoices.... Just so, I tell you, there will be more joy in heaven over one sinner who repents than over ninety-nine righteous persons who need no repentance."

LUKE 15:4–5, 7

Prayer

O Lord, bring us safely home on the shoulders of your love. Keep us from wandering off to places where it is difficult for you to find us. Amen.

Lenten Action

In honor of the lost sheep, seek out and forgive just one person for a slight or an indifference to you.

Saturday of the Fifth Week of Lent

THE MEANING OF DEATH AND LIFE

*D*eath is an affirmation of the purpose of life in an otherwise meaningless existence. The world could carry on its Godless plan if there were no death. What death is to an individual, that catastrophe is to civilization—the end of its wickedness. This is a source of anguish to the modern mind, for not only must human beings die, but the world must die. Death is a negative testimony to God's power in a meaningless world, for by it God brings meaningless existence to nought. Because God exists, evil cannot carry on its wickedness indefinitely. If there were no catastrophe, such as the Apocalypse reveals, at the end of the world, the universe would then be the triumph of chaos....

Death proves also that life has meaning, because it reveals that the virtues and goodness practiced within time do not find their completion except in eternity.

FULTON J. SHEEN, *THE POWER OF LOVE*

The Death and Resurrection of Lazarus

When Jesus arrived [at Bethany], he found that Lazarus [the brother of Martha and Mary] had already been in the tomb for four days.... Jesus...came to the tomb. It was a cave, and a stone was lying against it. Jesus said, "Take away the stone." Martha, the sister of the dead man, said to him, "Lord, already there is stench because he has been dead four days." Jesus said to her, "Did I not tell you that if you believed you would see the glory of God?" So they took away the stone.. And Jesus looked upward and said, "Father, I thank you for having heard me. I knew that you always hear me, but I have said this for the sake of the crowd standing here, so that they may believe that you sent me." When [Jesus] had said this, he cried with a loud voice, "Lazarus, come out!" The dead man came out, his hands and feet bound with strips of cloth, and his face wrapped in a cloth. So Jesus said to them, "Unbind him, and let him go."

JOHN 11:17, 38–44

Prayer

God of Eternal Wisdom, give us the strength to die to our sinful selves, to the ugly feelings, the discord of our daily lives so that we may live in kindness, good will, and charity in word and deed. Unbind our eyes so that we recall our blindness to our own sins, lest we forget the death that our sinfulness has caused you. Grant us growth in detachment from the evils of existence here on earth and give us instead the strength to be your steadfast disciples standing beneath the cross. Amen.

Lenten Action

Make an act of faith and hope in the reality of the yet invisible life of eternity and in the perpetual glory of God.

DAY 40

Passion Sunday (Palm Sunday)

OUR LORD'S LAST SABBATH

*I*f anybody asks you why you are untying it [the ass the disciples were sent to find], this must be your answer, 'The Lord has need of it'" (Lk 19:31). Perhaps no greater paradox was ever written than this—on the one hand the sovereignty of the Lord, and on the other hand his "need." This combination of Divinity and dependence, of possession and poverty was the consequence of the Word becoming flesh. Truly, he who was rich became poor for our sakes, that we might be rich. Our Lord borrowed a boat from a fisherman from which to preach; he borrowed barley loaves and fishes from a boy to feed the multitude; he borrowed a grave from which he would rise; and now he borrowed an ass on which to enter Jerusalem. Sometimes God preempts and requisitions the things of man, as if to remind him that everything is a gift from him.

FULTON J. SHEEN, *THE LIFE OF CHRIST*

JESUS' ENTRY INTO JERUSALEM

After throwing their cloaks on the colt, [the disciples] set Jesus on it. As he rode along, people kept spreading their cloaks on the road. As he was now approaching the path down from the Mount of Olives, the whole multitude of the disciples began to praise God joyfully with a loud voice for all the deeds of power that they had seen, saying, "Blessed is the king / who comes in the name of the Lord! / Peace in heaven, / and glory in the highest heaven!" Some of the Pharisees in the crowd said to him, "Teacher, order your disciples to stop." He answered, "I tell you, if these were silent, the stones would shout out."

LUKE 19:35–40

PRAYER

Prince of Peace, soften our hearts of stone so that even they can sing your glory. Amen.

LENTEN ACTION

Wear a sprig of greenery—of any kind available in your area—on your lapel or dress in order to commemorate the entry of our Lord into Jerusalem when those present tore down branches from trees to throw in his path. Alternately, in some countries, Palm Sunday is known as "Fig Sunday," and fig pudding or fresh figs are served at dinner on this day. Observe this custom if you wish.

DAY 41

Monday of Holy Week

THE LAST SUPPER

Since our Divine Lord came to die, it was fitting that there be a Memorial of his death. Since he was God, as well as man, and since he never spoke of his death without speaking of his Resurrection, should he not himself institute the precise memorial of his own death? And that is exactly what he did the night of the Last Supper….His Memorial was instituted, not because he would die and be buried, but because he would live again after the Resurrection. His Memorial would be the fulfillment of the Law and the prophets; it would be one in which there would be a Lamb sacrificed to commemorate spiritual freedom; above all, it would be a Memorial of a New Covenant…a Testament between God and man.

FULTON J. SHEEN, *THE LIFE OF CHRIST*

INSTITUTING THE EUCHARIST

When the hour came, [Jesus] took...a loaf of bread, and when he had given thanks, he broke it and gave it to [his apostles], saying, "This is my body, which is given for you. Do this in remembrance of me." And he did the same with the cup after supper, saying, "This cup that is poured out for you is the new covenant in my blood."

LUKE 22:14–20

PRAYER

Lord of the Eucharist, bring us out of our darkness and let us pray as did the prophet Malachi that this sacrifice will be enacted from the rising of the sun to its setting in your honor and for our sins. Amen.

LENTEN ACTION

Our Lord instituted the Eucharist at the Passover feast which itself was a commemoration of the preservation of the Israelites from the Egyptians. They escaped the purge of their firstborn sons by putting the blood of a lamb on their lintels. Put a representation of a lamb on your door or window as a reminder of Christ's sacrifice.

DAY 42

Tuesday of Holy Week

THE INNER CROSS

E very unhappy soul in the world has a cross embedded on it. The cross was never meant to be on the inside, but only on the outside. When the Israelites were bitten by the serpents, and the poison seeped within, Moses planted a brazen serpent on a stick and all who looked on it were healed….So the Son of Man came in the likeness of man, but was without sin, and all who look upon him on his cross are saved. In like manner, the inner cross disappears when one catches a vision of the great outer Cross on Calvary.

FULTON J. SHEEN, *PEACE OF SOUL*

THE AGONY IN THE GARDEN

[Jesus] came out and went, as was his custom, to the Mount of Olives; and the disciples followed him. When he reached the place, he said to them, "Pray that you may not come into the time of trial." Then he withdrew from them about a stone's throw, knelt down, and prayed, "Father, if you are willing, remove this cup from me; yet, not my will but yours be done." Then an angel from heaven appeared to him and gave him strength. In his anguish he prayed more earnestly, and his sweat became like great drops of blood falling down on the ground.

LUKE 22:39–44

PRAYER

Christ, ever faithful to the Father's will, strengthen us so that we may not fall into the sleep of indifference and deny you even as you take on the immense burden of our sins, both past, present, and future. Amen.

LENTEN ACTION

Pray for all those who have betrayed another, especially for those who have turned against relatives, friends, or neighbors.

DAY 43

Wednesday of Holy Week

THE SCOURGING AND THE CROWNING

Our Lord described himself as having a baptism wherewith he was to be baptized. John gave him the baptism of water, but the Roman soldiers gave him his baptism of blood. After opening his sacred flesh with violent stripes, they now put on him a purple robe which adhered to his bleeding body. Then they plaited a crown of thorns which they placed on his head. They mocked him and put a rod in his hand after beating him on the head. Then they knelt down before him in feigned adoration.

FULTON J. SHEEN, *LIFE OF CHRIST*

SMITTEN FOR OUR SINS

> *Surely he has borne our infirmities*
>   *and carried our diseases;*
> *yet we accounted him stricken,*
>   *struck down by God, and afflicted.*
> *But he was wounded for our transgressions,*
>   *crushed for our iniquities;*
> *upon him was the punishment that made us whole,*
>   *and by his bruises we are healed.*

ISAIAH 53:4–5

PRAYER

Lord Jesus Christ, you endured every torture at the hands of your enemies for the love of us who are now not always your friends. Open to us the light of your Resurrection and grant us the grace to walk out from the darkness of death into the light of eternity. Amen.

LENTEN ACTION

Wear black or purple today as a sign of solidarity with Christ's crucifixion and death.

DAY 44

Holy Thursday

THE CROSS

*M*any a cross we bear is of our own manufacture; we made it by our sins. But the cross which the Savior carried was not his, but ours. One beam in contradiction to another beam was the symbol of our will in contradiction to his own. To the women who met him on the roadway, he said: "Weep not for me." To shed tears for the dying Savior is to lament the remedy; it were wiser to lament the sin that caused it. If Innocence itself took a Cross, then how shall we, who are guilty, complain against it?

FULTON J. SHEEN, *THE WORLD'S FIRST LOVE*

PLEA FOR DELIVERANCE

My God, my God, why have you forsaken me...?
I am a worm, and not human;
   scorned by others, and despised by the people....
I am poured out like water,
   and all my bones are out of joint;
my heart is like wax;
   it is melted within my breast;
my mouth is dried up like a potsherd,
   and my tongue sticks to my jaws;
   you lay me in the dust of death.
For dogs are all around me;
   a company of evildoers encircles me.
My hands and feet have shriveled;
I can count all my bones.

PSALM 22:1, 6, 14–17

PRAYER

Lord Jesus Christ, in your sufferings on the cross, we have a sign of God's love and mercy in a language we can understand. Let us then not be afraid to lay down our own lives for our brothers and our sisters whatever form that sacrifice may take. Amen.

LENTEN ACTION

As a reminder of the three days preceding Easter—Holy Thursday, Good Friday, and Holy Saturday—set up a small holy altar in an appropriate place. This space could be a table holding a crucifix and three lighted candles. Leave this space intact for Holy Thursday and the following two days.

DAY 45

Good Friday

THE FIRE OF SIN

The green tree was Christ himself; the dry tree the world. He was the green tree of life transplanted from Eden; the dry tree was Jerusalem first, and then the unconverted world. If the Romans so treated him who was innocent, how would they treat the Truth that is in his Church; in an uneasy conscience perhaps he beckoned you to his confessional; in a passing prayer he called you to greater prayerfulness....You accepted the truth, you confessed your sins, you perfected your spiritual life, and lo! in those moments when you thought you were losing everything, you found everything; when you thought you were going into your grave, you were walking in the newness of life....The antiphon of the Empty Tomb was striking on the chords of your heart. It was not you who died; it was sin. It was not Christ who died; it was death.

FULTON J. SHEEN, *THE ETERNAL GALILEAN*

BE AS UNLEAVENED BREAD

Do you not know that a little yeast leavens the whole batch of dough? Clean out the old yeast so that you may be a new batch, as you really are unleavened. For our paschal lamb, Christ, has been sacrificed. Therefore, let us celebrate the festival, not with the old yeast, the yeast of malice and evil, but with the unleavened bread of sincerity and truth.

1 CORINTHIANS 5:6–8

PRAYER

Lord God, ever-loving Father, we know that your risen Son resides with you in heaven, interceding for us in his boundless mercy. We acknowledge his Resurrection and sing praise to him who has endured the cross and the grave. Amen. Alleluia!

LENTEN ACTION

At the time of Christ, the science behind the action of yeast as a leavening agent was unknown; thus, yeast was sometimes considered to be the work of the devil. Pledge to throw out the old yeast of evil, replacing it with the yeastless bread of sincerity and truth, making sure that your conduct is consistent with a commitment to Christ.

DAY 46

Holy Saturday

OUR MOTHER OF MERCY

Through the centuries the Church Fathers have said that Our Lord keeps for himself half his regency, which is the kingdom of justice, but the other half he gives away to his Mother, and this is the kingdom of mercy. At the marriage feast of Cana, Our Lord said that the hour of his Passion was not yet at hand—the hour when justice would be fulfilled. But his Blessed Mother begged him not to wait, but to be merciful to those who were in need, and to supply their wants by changing water into wine. Three years later, when not the water was changed into wine, but the wine into blood, he fulfilled all justice, but surrendered half his kingdom by giving to us that which no one else could give, namely, his Mother: "Behold thy Mother." Whatever mothers do for sons, that his Mother would do for us, and more.

FULTON J. SHEEN, *THE WORLD'S FIRST LOVE*

BURIAL OF JESUS

Now there was a good and righteous man named Joseph, who, though a member of the council, had not agreed to their plan and action. He came from the Jewish town of Arimathea, and he was waiting expectantly for the kingdom of God. This man went to Pilate and asked for the body of Jesus. Then he took it down, wrapped it in a linen cloth, and laid it in a rock-hewn tomb where no one had ever been laid. It was the day of Preparation, and the sabbath was beginning. The women who had come with him from Galilee followed, and they saw the tomb and how his body was laid. Then they returned, and prepared spices and ointments.

On the sabbath they rested according to the commandment.

LUKE 23:50–56

PRAYER

Say the prayer of Saint Bernard to Mary, Queen of Mercy and Mother of Sinners: Recite the *Memorare* in prayerful hope of Mary's aid in seeking forgiveness.

LENTEN ACTION

On the Easter vigil in some countries, bonfires are lit in anticipation of Easter day. In other countries, Easter Saturday is an occasion of housecleaning in anticipation of the arrival of spring. Light a small fire in your fireplace or clean one small area of your desk or home or spend time preparing Easter letters to friends.

PART II

READINGS for EASTER WEEK

DAY 47

Easter Sunday

THE NEW DYNAMICS OF EASTER

*F*inally the Easter lesson comes to our own lives. It has been suggested…that it is better to go down to defeat in the love of the Cross than to win the passing victory of a world that crucified.

And now it is suggested in conclusion that it is better to go down to defeat in the eyes of the world by giving to God that which is wholly and totally ours. If we give God our energy, we give him back his own gift; if we give him our talents, our joys, and our possessions, we return to him that which he placed in our hands not as owners but as mere trustees.

FULTON J. SHEEN, *THE ELECTRONIC CHRISTIAN*

A New Goal

Whatever gains I [Paul] had, these I have come to regard as loss because of Christ….For his sake I have suffered the loss of all things, and I regard them as rubbish, in order that I may gain Christ and be found in him, not having a righteousness of my own that comes from the law, but one that comes through faith in Christ….I want to know Christ and the power of his resurrection.

PHILIPPIANS 3:7–10

Prayer

Risen Lord, we sing with joy today on your resurrection and see it as a sign of our success in winning our salvation. We pray to always recognize this victory and not to put it aside in the problems of daily existence. Amen.

Easter Action

Formerly in Hungry, young men set up Easter trees decorated with painted eggs. Decorate a small Easter tree of your own with friendship eggs and ribbons of many colors. Hang an egg in gratitude for each gift you have received this Lenten season.

DAY 48

Easter Monday

ETERNITY OF EASTER

Our Blessed Savior revealed to Mary Magdalen the truth that he was no longer to be seen under the form of time and in the world of sensations, but only by the soul and in the world of eternity....This great truth needs to be stressed strongly on this new Easter Day when human beings no longer speak of eternity, but only of time; when they are more concerned about citizenship in the Kingdom of this world than citizenship in the Kingdom of Heaven; when their interests center more about passing questions of science, politics, economics, wealth, and power, instead of around the Risen Christ who sits eternally at the right hand of God.

FULTON J. SHEEN, *MANIFESTATIONS OF CHRIST*

NEW LIFE IN CHRIST

So if you have been raised with Christ, seek those things that are above, where Christ is seated at the right hand of God. Set your minds on things that are above, not on things that are on earth, for you have died, and your life is hidden with Christ in God. When Christ who is your life is revealed, then you also will be revealed with him in glory.

COLOSSIANS 3:1–4

PRAYER

Say this prayer written by Bishop Sheen: *May our souls be flooded with the peace and joy which comes from the victory of the Risen Christ, who bears now and forevermore not wounds, but scars as pledges of his love and forgiveness.*

EASTER ACTION

Signify a new life in the Risen Christ by choosing one small compromise or one small selfish habit to forego as a symbol of renewal.

DAY 49

Easter Tuesday

KEPT FOR ALL ETERNITY

*T*he human heart is not shaped like a valentine heart, perfect and regular in contour; it is slightly irregular in shape as if a small piece of it were missing out of its side. The missing part may very well symbolize a piece that a spear tore out of the universal heart of Humanity on the Cross, but it probably symbolizes something more. It may very well mean that when God created each human heart, he kept a small sample of it in heaven, and sent the rest of it into the world, where it would each day learn the lesson that it could never be really happy, that is could never be really wholly in love, that it could never be really wholehearted until it rested with the Risen Christ in an eternal Easter.

FULTON J. SHEEN, *MANIFESTATIONS OF CHRIST*

TESTIMONY OF TRUTH

There are three things that testify: the Spirit and the water and the blood, and these three agree. If we receive human testimony, the testimony of God is greater; for this is the testimony of God that he has testified to his Son. Those who believe in the Son of God have the testimony of their hearts....And this is the testimony: God gave us eternal life, and this life is in his Son. Whoever has the Son has life; whoever does not have the Son of God does not have life.

1 JOHN 5:7–12

PRAYER

Risen Lord, grant us the grace to nurture the life we receive through the pledge of your Easter Resurrection. Protect us from the false idols of the world and lead us to that Eternal Easter with you in heaven. Amen.

EASTER ACTION

Set up the empty manger from your Christmas crèche or the vacant stable as a reminder of the reality of the Resurrection.

DAY 50

Easter Wednesday

MARK OF THE CREATOR

God writes his name on the soul of every person. Reason and conscience are the God within us in the natural order.... Human beings are like so many books issuing from the Divine press, and if nothing else be written on them, at least the name of the Author is indissolubly engraved on the title page. God is like the watermark on paper, which may be written over without ever being obscured.

FULTON J. SHEEN, *LIFE OF CHRIST*

TREE OF LIFE

The angel showed me the river of the water of life, bright as crystal, flowing from the throne of God and of the Lamb through the middle of the street of the city. On either side of the river is the tree of life with its twelve kinds of fruit, producing its fruit each month; and the leaves of the tree are for the healing of nations. Nothing accursed will be found there any more. But the throne of God and of the Lamb will be in it, and his servants will worship him; they will see his face, and his name will be on their foreheads.

REVELATION 22:1–5

PRAYER

Dear God, tree of all life, we are thankful to find ourselves in the new Garden of Eden where your blood shed on the cross may give us access to abundant and eternal life. We wait for that day and hope in your kindness to deliver us from sin. Amen.

EASTER ACTION

Plan a visit to a local botanical garden to admire the trees of God's creation. In some cultures, new babies are gifted with a silver pot in which a sapling is planted. Plant an Easter tree today in honor of Christ's Resurrection.

Easter Thursday

PASSING BY

*E*very word that comes to us about the uncomfortable, the homeless, the lepers, is the Son of God passing by. If we let him pass, he may never be recalled. Graces unused are not often repeated; whispers ignored do not become shouts. All through life, our hands will stretch forth empty of the richest blessings of wisdom and truth unless they are first used to clutch as the sleeve of the Divine who "makes as if he would pass us by."

FULTON J. SHEEN, *GUIDE TO CONTENTMENT*

ROAD TO EMMAUS

Two of the [disciples] were going to a village called Emmaus....While they were talking and discussing, Jesus himself came near and went with them, but their eyes were kept from recognizing him. And he said to them, "What are you discussing with each other while you walk along?" They stood still, looking sad. Then one of them, whose name was Cleopas, answered him, "Are you the only stranger in Jerusalem who does not know the things that have taken place there in these days?" He asked them, "What things?" They replied, "The things about Jesus of Nazareth, who was a prophet mighty in deed and word before God and all the people, and how our chief priests and leaders handed him over to be condemned to death and crucified him."

...As they came near the village to which they were going, he walked ahead as if he were going on. But they urged him strongly, saying, "Stay with us, because it is almost evening and the day is now nearly over." So he went in to stay with them.

LUKE 24:13, 15–20, 28–29

PRAYER

Risen Lord, help us to recognize and avoid the false Christs who say "Here I am," and instead to have the enlightened eyes of faith to see you passing by in the poor, the afflicted, the persecuted. Let us see you in them and let us act to help them. Amen.

EASTER ACTION

Think back and record the times when you were like the unseeing disciples "on the road to Emmaus." Meditate on how you would handle things differently now.

Day 52

Easter Friday

BREAKING THE BONDS OF DEATH

What is most peculiar about Easter is that although the followers of Jesus had heard him say he would break the bonds of death, when he actually did, no one believed it….The followers were not expecting a Resurrection and, therefore, did not imagine they saw something of which they were ardently hoping. Even Mary Magdalene, who within that very week had been told about the Resurrection when she saw her own brother raised to life from a grave, did not believe it. She came on Sunday morning to the tomb with spices to anoint a body—not to greet a Risen Savior. On the way, the question of the women was: "Who will roll back the stone?" Their problem was how they could get in; not whether the Savior would get out.

FULTON J. SHEEN, *WAY TO INNER PEACE*

THE DOUBTER

Thomas (who was called the Twin), one of the twelve, was not with them [the disciples] when Jesus came. So the other disciples told him, "We have seen the Lord," but he said to them, "Unless I see the mark of the nails in his hands, and put my finger in the mark of the nails and my hand in his side, I will not believe."

JOHN 20:24–25

PRAYER

Lord Jesus Christ, give us your saving love and erase all our doubts about your victory on the incongruous altar of the cross. Give us gentle fear, not full-blown panic, so we may awakened from the sleep of sin. Amen.

EASTER ACTION

Put some nails in your pocket or purse to remind you of your tendency to doubt your faith.

DAY 53

Easter Saturday

LOVE AS GIFT

*O*n the Sunday after the Resurrection, early in the morning, seven men were out fishing in a boat. One of those men, Peter, three times had denied the Divine Master. Three times he was asked if he loved, twice in a very sacrificial way, and the other in a human way. When all three questions were answered in the affirmative, there came the command to feed lambs, sheep, and firstlings of the flock. In other words, love is the condition of service.

We are knit to the Fountain [of Love] by true affection, which is based upon the consciousness of our falls, our weaknesses, and also our reception of his forgiving mercy. Then we shall have the qualities that fit us in the impulse to serve and help our fellow human beings.

FULTON J. SHEEN, *FOOTPRINTS IN A DARKENED FOREST*

CAST YOUR NETS WHERE I TELL YOU

[After his Resurrection], Jesus showed himself again to the disciples by the Sea of Tiberias; and he showed himself in this way....Just after daybreak, Jesus stood on the beach.... [The disciples] saw a charcoal fire there, with fish on it, and bread. Jesus said to them..., "Come and have breakfast."

When they had finished breakfast, Jesus said to Simon Peter, "Simon son of John, do you love me more than these?" He said to him, "Yes, Lord; you know that I love you." Jesus said to him, "Feed my lambs."

JOHN 21:1, 4, 9, 12, 15

PRAYER

God of Utmost Generosity, remind us that after we share the Eucharist we may always acknowledge that your love is alive in us and that we must in turn "feed" all with the Good News of Christ. Remind us to follow you will even as we serve others. Amen.

EASTER ACTION

Be a true Easter person and find joy in every event of the day ahead.

Second Sunday of Easter

THE HOPE OF EASTER

The Cross had asked the questions; the Resurrection had answered them....The Cross had asked: "Why does God permit evil and sin to nail Justice to a tree?" The Resurrection answered: "That sin, having done its worst, might exhaust itself and thus be overcome by Love that is stronger than either sin or death."

Thus there emerges the Easter lesson that the power of evil and the chaos of any one moment can be defied and conquered, for the basis of our hope is not in any construct of human power but in the power of God, who has given to the evil of this earth its one mortal wound—an open tomb, a gaping sepulcher, an empty grave.

FULTON J. SHEEN, *CROSS-WAYS*

JESUS IS LIFE

Jesus said, "I am the resurrection and the life. Those who believe in me, even though they die, will live, and everyone who lives and believes in me will never die."

JOHN 11:25–26

PRAYER

Most High God, you who taught us how to suffer, who showed us the example of humility, who demonstrated obedience even unto death, we are awed by your example. Let us bear our own suffering willingly, let us find true humility our hearts, and let us happily submit to obedience to you law. Amen.

EASTER ACTION

Choose one of the commandments to keep faithfully and in its true spirit for the next week. Make the keeping of this commandment a series of positive acts.

Sources and Acknowledgments

"God, in his great mercy…," page 2, *A Catholic Catechism* by Archbishop Fulton J. Sheen, Conference on "Sin," published in twenty-five CD-Roms by Keep the Faith, Ramsey, New Jersey, no date.

"The worse sinners are…," page 4, *A Catholic Catechism* by Archbishop Fulton J. Sheen, Conference on "Sin," published in twenty-five CD-Roms by Keep the Faith, Ramsey, New Jersey.

"Well, why breathe? We have…," page 6, *A Catholic Catechism* by Archbishop Fulton J. Sheen, Conference on "Prayer Is a Dialogue," published in twenty-five CD-Roms by Keep the Faith, Ramsey, New Jersey.

"Mortification is good, but only when…," page 8, *Peace of Soul*, Liguori, Mo.: Liguori/Triumph, Republished 1996.

"The nature of giving is best illustrated…," page 10, *Footprints in a Darkened Forest*, New York: Meredith Press, 1967.

"Decisions and resolutions taken…," page 12, *Guide to Contentment*, New York: Maco Publishing Company, 1967.

"Why should we turn the other cheek? Because…," page 14, *Life of Christ*, New York: McGraw-Hill Book Company, Inc., 1958.

"When you fail to measure up…," page 16, *Preface to Religion*, New York: P. J. Kenedy & Sons, 1946.

"God will not do what…," page 18, *Lift Up Your Heart: A Guide to Spiritual Peace*, Liguori, Mo.: Liguori/Triumph, Republished 1997.

"If you want to know about God…," page 20, *Preface to Religion*, New York: P. J. Kenedy & Sons, 1946.

"There was a beautiful monotony…," page 22, *Manifestations of Christ*, Washington, D.C.: National Conference of Catholic Men, 1932.

"Darkness may be creative, for it…," page 24, *Cross-Ways*, Garden City, N.Y.: Doubleday/Image, 1984.

"Judging our fellow human beings…," page 26, *Guide to Contentment*, New York: Maco Publishing Company, 1967.

"There are certain psychological…," page 28, *Way to Inner Peace*, New York: Garden City Books, 1955.

"When the Light shines…," page 30, *Life of Christ*, New York: McGraw-Hill Book Company, Inc., 1958.

"This is probably the most talkative…," page 32, *Lift Up Your Heart: A Guide to Spiritual Peace*, Liguori, Mo.: Liguori/Triumph, Republished 1997.

"Love has three and only three…," page 34, *The Eternal Galilean*, New York: D. Appleton-Century Company, Inc., 1934.

"Because kindness is related to…," page 36, *Way to Happiness*, New York: Garden City Books, 1954.

"The Church believes that…," page 38, *Manifestations of Christ*, Washington, D.C.: National Conference of Catholic Men, 1932.

"Cheer may be natural, in which…," page 40, *Simple Truths: Thinking Life Through With Fulton J. Sheen*, Ligouri, Mo.: Liguori/Triumph, 1998.

"There is a law that is not…," page 42, *Guide to Contentment*, New York: Maco Publishing Company, 1967.

"Messages came to many in the…," page 44, *Rejoice*, Garden City, N.Y.: Doubleday/Image, 1984.

"The executioners expected Jesus to…," page 46, *Life of Christ*, New York: McGraw-Hill Book Company, Inc., 1958.

"Moses and Cain each hid his face…," page 48, *Lift Up Your Heart: A Guide to Spiritual Peace*, Liguori, Mo.: Liguori/Triumph, Republished 1997.

"From twelve o'clock until three…," page 50, *Life of Christ*, New York: McGraw-Hill Book Company, Inc., 1958.

"Along with silence, there…," page 52, *Simple Truths: Thinking Life Through With Fulton J. Sheen*, Ligouri, Mo.: Liguori/Triumph, 1998.

"Our Blessed Lord said...," page 54, *Manifestations of Christ*, Washington, D.C.: National Conference of Catholic Men, 1932.

"Almost the first word of Our Lord's...," page 56, *Footprints in a Darkened Forest*, New York: Meredith Press, 1967.

"Love and Sacrifice go together...," page 58, *Footprints in a Darkened Forest*, New York: Meredith Press, 1967.

"We have this queer combination of...," page 60, *A Catholic Catechism* by Archbishop Fulton J. Sheen, Conference on "Christ in the Creed," published in twenty-five CD-Roms by Keep the Faith, Ramsey, New Jersey.

"Sorrow [for sins] is and intention to...," page 62, *A Catholic Catechism* by Archbishop Fulton J. Sheen, Conference on "Penance," published in twenty-five CD-Roms by Keep the Faith, Ramsey, New Jersey.

"If a man is ever to enjoy..." page 64, *The Moral Universe: A Preface to Christian Living*, Milwaukee: The Bruce Publishing Company, 1936.

"But though men failed in this crisis...," page 66, *The Seven Virtues*, New York: P. J. Kenedy & Sons, 1940.

"The only answer to the mystery of death...," page 68, *Footprints in a Darkened Forest*, New York: Meredith Press, 1967.

"In the beautiful Divine economy...," page 70, *Life of Christ*, New York: McGraw-Hill Book Company, Inc., 1958.

"The God-Man, who threw...," page 72, *The Seven Last Words*, New York: The Century Co., 1933.

"Sanctity is not a question...," page 74, *Manifestations of Christ*, Washington, D.C.: National Conference of Catholic Men, 1932.

"God solicits each of us...," page 76, *Lift Up Your Heart: A Guide to Spiritual Peace*, Liguori, Mo.: Liguori/Triumph, Republished 1997.

"Death is an affirmation...," page 78, *The Power of Love*, New York: Simon and Schuster, 1965.

"'If anybody asks...,'" page 80, *Life of Christ*, New York: McGraw-Hill Book Company, Inc., 1958.

"Since our Divine Lord came…," page 82, *Life of Christ*, New York: McGrawHill Book Company, Inc., 1958.

"Every unhappy soul…," page 84, *Peace of Soul*, Liguori, Mo.: Liguori/Triumph, republished 1996, original copyright 1949, New York: McGraw-Hill.

"Our Lord described himself…," page 86, *Life of Christ*, New York: McGraw-Hill Book Company, Inc., 1958.

"Many a cross we bear…," page 88, *The World's First Love*, New York: McGraw-Hill Book Company, Inc., 1952.

"The green tree was Christ…," page 90, *The Eternal Galilean*, New York: D. Appleton-Century Company, Inc., 1934.

"Through the centuries the Church…," page 92, *The World's First Love*, New York: McGraw-Hill Book Company, Inc., 1952.

"Finally the Easter lesson…," page 96, *The Moral Universe: A Preface to Christian Living*, Milwaukee: The Bruce Publishing Company, 1936.

"The Blessed Savior revealed to…," page 98, *Manifestations of Christ*, Washington, D.C.: National Conference of Catholic Men, 1932.

"The human heart is not shaped…," page 100, *Manifestations of Christ*, Washington, D.C.: National Conference of Catholic Men, 1932.

"God writes his name…," page 102, *Life of Christ*, New York: McGraw-Hill Book Company, Inc., 1958.

"Every word that comes…," page 104, *Guide to Contentment*, New York: Maco Publishing Company, 1967.

"What is most peculiar about Easter…," page 106, *Way to Inner Peace*, Garden City, New York: Garden City Books, 1955.

"On the Sunday after the Resurrection…," page 108, *Footprints in a Darkened Forest*, New York: Meredith Press, 1967.

"The Cross has asked the…," page 110, *Cross-Ways*, Garden City, N.Y.: Doubleday/Image, 1984.